EMMANUEL JOSEPH

The Emotionally Intelligent Entrepreneur, Blending Innovation, Culture, and Ethical Leadership

Copyright © 2025 by Emmanuel Joseph

All rights reserved. No part of this publication may be reproduced, stored or transmitted in any form or by any means, electronic, mechanical, photocopying, recording, scanning, or otherwise without written permission from the publisher. It is illegal to copy this book, post it to a website, or distribute it by any other means without permission.

First edition

This book was professionally typeset on Reedsy.
Find out more at reedsy.com

Contents

1	Chapter 1: The Roots of Emotional Intelligence	1
2	Chapter 2: The Intersection of Innovation and Emotional...	3
3	Chapter 3: Building a Culture of Emotional Intelligence	5
4	Chapter 4: Ethical Leadership and Emotional Intelligence	7
5	Chapter 5: The Role of Emotional Intelligence in...	9
6	Chapter 6: Emotional Intelligence in Team Dynamics	11
7	Chapter 7: The Impact of Emotional Intelligence on...	13
8	Chapter 8: Emotional Intelligence in Crisis Management	15
9	Chapter 9: Emotional Intelligence in Customer Relationships	17
10	Chapter 10: Emotional Intelligence in Negotiation and...	19
11	Chapter 11: The Role of Emotional Intelligence in Personal...	21
12	Chapter 12: Emotional Intelligence in Work-Life Balance	23
13	Chapter 13: Emotional Intelligence in Diversity and...	25
14	Chapter 14: Emotional Intelligence in Ethical...	27
15	Chapter 15: The Impact of Emotional Intelligence on...	29
16	Chapter 16: Emotional Intelligence in Strategic Planning	31
17	Chapter 17: The Future of Emotional Intelligence in...	33

1

Chapter 1: The Roots of Emotional Intelligence

Emotional intelligence (EI) is often hailed as a crucial ingredient for effective leadership. Unlike traditional intelligence measured by IQ, EI involves a deeper understanding of one's own emotions and the emotions of others. It comprises self-awareness, self-regulation, motivation, empathy, and social skills. These traits enable entrepreneurs to navigate complex social landscapes, build strong relationships, and lead with empathy and understanding. In an ever-evolving business environment, emotionally intelligent leaders are better equipped to inspire and engage their teams, driving innovation and fostering a positive organizational culture.

Entrepreneurs with high EI can recognize their emotional triggers and manage their reactions effectively. This self-regulation prevents impulsive decisions and promotes thoughtful, strategic thinking. Additionally, self-aware entrepreneurs are more attuned to their strengths and weaknesses, allowing them to leverage their talents while seeking support in areas where they may lack expertise. This balanced approach to self-improvement and humility fosters a growth mindset, essential for entrepreneurial success.

The importance of motivation in EI cannot be overstated. Entrepreneurs with a strong drive to achieve their goals are more resilient in the face of setbacks and challenges. They possess an intrinsic passion for their work, which fuels their determination and perseverance. This internal motivation not only propels them forward but also inspires their teams to strive for excellence. By fostering a culture of shared purpose and commitment, emotionally intelligent entrepreneurs can create a thriving, innovative work environment.

Empathy and social skills are the cornerstones of emotionally intelligent leadership. Entrepreneurs who can understand and connect with the emotions of others are better equipped to build trust and rapport with their teams, clients, and partners. Effective communication, active listening, and conflict resolution are essential social skills that enable entrepreneurs to navigate interpersonal dynamics with grace and tact. By cultivating a supportive and inclusive culture, emotionally intelligent leaders can harness the collective potential of their teams, driving innovation and success.

2

Chapter 2: The Intersection of Innovation and Emotional Intelligence

Innovation is the lifeblood of entrepreneurship, and emotionally intelligent entrepreneurs are uniquely positioned to drive groundbreaking ideas and solutions. Emotional intelligence enhances an entrepreneur's ability to identify and seize opportunities, fostering a mindset of curiosity and continuous learning. By embracing change and uncertainty, emotionally intelligent leaders can inspire their teams to think creatively and push the boundaries of what is possible.

One of the key aspects of innovation is the ability to empathize with customers and understand their needs. Emotionally intelligent entrepreneurs can tap into their empathy to gain valuable insights into customer pain points and preferences. This deep understanding allows them to develop products and services that truly resonate with their target audience, creating lasting value and competitive advantage. By putting themselves in their customers' shoes, emotionally intelligent leaders can anticipate market trends and stay ahead of the curve.

Collaboration is another critical component of innovation. Emotionally intelligent entrepreneurs excel at fostering a collaborative environment where diverse perspectives are valued and encouraged. By creating a culture of open communication and mutual respect, these leaders can harness the collective intelligence of their teams to drive innovation. They recognize the importance of psychological safety, ensuring that team members feel comfortable sharing their ideas and taking risks without fear of judgment or retribution.

Emotional intelligence also plays a vital role in managing the inevitable challenges and setbacks that come with innovation. Emotionally intelligent entrepreneurs can navigate these obstacles with resilience and composure, maintaining a positive outlook and inspiring their teams to persevere. By acknowledging and addressing the emotional impact of failure, these leaders can foster a growth mindset and encourage their teams to learn from their mistakes. This adaptability and resilience are essential for sustaining innovation in the face of adversity.

3

Chapter 3: Building a Culture of Emotional Intelligence

A strong organizational culture is the foundation of any successful enterprise, and emotionally intelligent entrepreneurs understand the importance of fostering a culture that prioritizes emotional well-being. By promoting a supportive and inclusive environment, these leaders can create a workplace where employees feel valued, motivated, and empowered to contribute their best work. A culture of emotional intelligence not only enhances employee satisfaction and retention but also drives productivity and innovation.

The first step in building an emotionally intelligent culture is to lead by example. Entrepreneurs who demonstrate self-awareness, empathy, and effective communication set the tone for their organization. By modeling emotionally intelligent behaviors, leaders can inspire their teams to adopt these practices and create a ripple effect throughout the organization. This leadership by example fosters a sense of trust and respect, laying the groundwork for a positive and collaborative work environment.

Emotionally intelligent entrepreneurs also prioritize the well-being of their employees. They recognize that a healthy work-life balance is essential for maintaining high levels of engagement and productivity. By offering flexible work arrangements, promoting mental health initiatives, and encouraging regular breaks, these leaders create a supportive environment where employees can thrive. This focus on well-being not only enhances job satisfaction but also reduces stress and burnout, leading to a more resilient and motivated workforce.

Effective communication is another cornerstone of an emotionally intelligent culture. Entrepreneurs who prioritize open and transparent communication create a climate of trust and psychological safety. By actively listening to their employees, providing constructive feedback, and encouraging open dialogue, these leaders can address concerns and resolve conflicts before they escalate. This proactive approach to communication fosters a sense of belonging and collaboration, driving innovation and team cohesion.

4

Chapter 4: Ethical Leadership and Emotional Intelligence

Ethical leadership is a critical aspect of emotional intelligence, and emotionally intelligent entrepreneurs understand the importance of aligning their values with their actions. By prioritizing ethical decision-making and demonstrating integrity, these leaders can build a strong reputation and earn the trust of their stakeholders. Ethical leadership not only enhances an organization's credibility but also fosters a positive and sustainable business environment.

Emotionally intelligent entrepreneurs are guided by a strong sense of purpose and values. They recognize the importance of ethical considerations in their decision-making processes and strive to balance profit with social responsibility. By adhering to ethical principles, these leaders can create long-term value for their organization and society. This commitment to ethical leadership fosters a culture of accountability and transparency, where employees feel empowered to act with integrity.

Transparency and honesty are essential components of ethical leadership. Emotionally intelligent entrepreneurs prioritize open communication and ensure that their actions align with their words. By being transparent about their decision-making processes and acknowledging their mistakes, these leaders can build trust and credibility with their stakeholders. This honesty and accountability create a culture of trust, where employees feel confident in their leaders' ability to make ethical decisions.

Ethical leadership also involves prioritizing the well-being of all stakeholders, including employees, customers, and the broader community. Emotionally intelligent entrepreneurs recognize that their actions have far-reaching impacts and strive to create positive outcomes for all. By promoting social and environmental responsibility, these leaders can contribute to a more sustainable and equitable world. This commitment to ethical leadership not only enhances an organization's reputation but also drives long-term success and resilience.

5

Chapter 5: The Role of Emotional Intelligence in Decision-Making

Decision-making is a critical aspect of entrepreneurship, and emotional intelligence plays a vital role in this process. Emotionally intelligent entrepreneurs can navigate complex and uncertain situations with clarity and confidence, making informed decisions that align with their values and goals. By leveraging their emotional awareness and empathy, these leaders can consider the perspectives and needs of all stakeholders, ensuring that their decisions are fair and balanced.

Self-awareness is the foundation of emotionally intelligent decision-making. Entrepreneurs who are in tune with their emotions can recognize when their feelings may be influencing their judgment. This awareness allows them to take a step back and evaluate the situation objectively, ensuring that their decisions are based on rational thinking rather than emotional impulses. By managing their emotions effectively, these leaders can make more thoughtful and strategic decisions.

Empathy is another crucial component of emotionally intelligent decision-making. Entrepreneurs who can understand and consider the emotions and perspectives of others are better equipped to make decisions that benefit all stakeholders. By putting themselves in the shoes of their employees, customers, and partners, these leaders can anticipate the potential impact of their decisions and make choices that are fair and considerate. This empathetic approach to decision-making fosters trust and collaboration, driving long-term success.

Emotional intelligence also enhances an entrepreneur's ability to manage stress and uncertainty. In high-pressure situations, emotionally intelligent leaders can maintain their composure and think clearly, making decisions that are informed and deliberate. By staying calm and focused, these leaders can navigate challenges with resilience and confidence, inspiring their teams to do the same. This ability to manage stress and uncertainty is essential for sustaining entrepreneurial success in a dynamic and rapidly changing business environment.

6

Chapter 6: Emotional Intelligence in Team Dynamics

Team dynamics are a critical aspect of organizational success, and emotionally intelligent entrepreneurs understand the importance of fostering a positive and cohesive team environment. By leveraging their emotional intelligence, these leaders can build strong relationships, resolve conflicts, and create a culture of collaboration and mutual support. This focus on team dynamics not only enhances productivity and innovation but also drives employee satisfaction and retention.

Effective communication is the cornerstone of positive team dynamics. Entrepreneurs who prioritize open and transparent communication create a climate of trust and psychological safety. By actively listening to their team members, providing constructive feedback, and encouraging open dialogue, these leaders can address concerns and resolve conflicts before they escalate. This proactive approach to communication fosters a sense of belonging and collaboration, driving team cohesion and productivity.

Emotionally intelligent entrepreneurs also recognize the importance of empathy in team dynamics. By understanding and valuing the emotions and perspectives of their team members, these leaders can create an inclusive and supportive work environment. This empathy allows them to build strong relationships and foster a sense of trust and respect within the team. By valuing diversity and encouraging open dialogue, emotionally intelligent leaders can harness the collective potential of their teams, driving innovation and success.

Conflict resolution is another critical aspect of team dynamics, and emotionally intelligent entrepreneurs excel at navigating interpersonal conflicts with grace and tact. By addressing conflicts promptly and constructively, these leaders can prevent issues from escalating and maintain a positive team environment. This focus on conflict resolution fosters a culture of accountability and mutual respect, where team members feel comfortable expressing their concerns and working together to find solutions.

7

Chapter 7: The Impact of Emotional Intelligence on Leadership Styles

Leadership styles vary widely, and emotionally intelligent entrepreneurs can adapt their approach to suit the needs of their teams and organizations. By leveraging their emotional intelligence, these leaders can strike a balance between authoritative, democratic, and transformational leadership styles, creating a dynamic and responsive work environment. This adaptability not only enhances their effectiveness as leaders but also drives employee engagement and performance.

Authoritative leadership involves setting clear expectations and providing direction, while also empowering employees to take ownership of their work. Emotionally intelligent entrepreneurs can use their self-awareness and empathy to communicate their vision and goals effectively, inspiring their teams to achieve their best. By providing support and guidance, these leaders can foster a sense of autonomy and accountability, driving innovation and productivity.

Democratic leadership emphasizes collaboration and participation, allowing team members to contribute their ideas and perspectives. Emotionally intelligent entrepreneurs excel at fostering open communication and mutual respect, creating a culture of inclusivity and shared decision-making. By valuing the input of their team members, these leaders can harness the collective intelligence of their organization, driving innovation and problem-solving.

Transformational leadership involves inspiring and motivating employees to achieve their full potential. Emotionally intelligent entrepreneurs can use their empathy and social skills to connect with their team members on a deeper level, understanding their individual strengths and aspirations. By providing mentorship and support, these leaders can create a culture of continuous learning and growth, driving long-term success and resilience.

8

Chapter 8: Emotional Intelligence in Crisis Management

Crisis management is a critical aspect of entrepreneurship, and emotionally intelligent leaders are uniquely equipped to navigate challenging situations with grace and composure. By leveraging their emotional intelligence, these leaders can maintain a sense of calm and control, making informed decisions that prioritize the well-being of their organization and stakeholders. This ability to manage crises effectively not only enhances their credibility as leaders but also drives organizational resilience and recovery.

During a crisis, emotionally intelligent entrepreneurs can use their self-awareness to recognize and manage their stress and emotions. By staying calm and focused, these leaders can think clearly and make rational decisions, even in high-pressure situations. This composure not only enhances their decision-making abilities but also inspires confidence and trust among their team members and stakeholders.

Empathy is another crucial component of effective crisis management. Emotionally intelligent entrepreneurs can understand and address the emotional impact of a crisis on their employees, customers, and partners. By providing support and reassurance, these leaders can foster a sense of solidarity and resilience, helping their organization navigate the challenges and uncertainties of a crisis. This empathetic approach to crisis management enhances trust and loyalty, driving long-term success and recovery.

Effective communication is essential during a crisis, and emotionally intelligent entrepreneurs excel at maintaining open and transparent communication with their stakeholders. By providing regular updates and addressing concerns promptly, these leaders can keep their teams informed and engaged, minimizing uncertainty and confusion. This proactive approach to communication fosters a sense of trust and collaboration, driving organizational resilience and recovery.

9

Chapter 9: Emotional Intelligence in Customer Relationships

Customer relationships are the cornerstone of business success, and emotionally intelligent entrepreneurs understand the importance of building and maintaining strong connections with their customers. By leveraging their emotional intelligence, these leaders can create personalized and meaningful experiences that resonate with their target audience, driving customer loyalty and satisfaction.

Empathy is a critical component of building strong customer relationships. Emotionally intelligent entrepreneurs can put themselves in their customers' shoes, understanding their needs, preferences, and pain points. This deep understanding allows them to develop products and services that truly meet their customers' expectations, creating lasting value and competitive advantage. By demonstrating empathy and genuine concern for their customers, these leaders can build trust and loyalty, driving long-term success.

Effective communication is another essential aspect of customer relationships. Emotionally intelligent entrepreneurs can use their social skills to engage with their customers in a meaningful and authentic way. By actively listening to their feedback, addressing their concerns, and providing timely and personalized responses, these leaders can create a positive and memorable customer experience. This focus on effective communication enhances customer satisfaction and drives brand loyalty.

Emotionally intelligent entrepreneurs also recognize the importance of ethical behavior in customer relationships. By prioritizing honesty, transparency, and integrity, these leaders can build a strong reputation and earn the trust of their customers. This commitment to ethical behavior not only enhances customer relationships but also drives long-term business success and sustainability.

10

Chapter 10: Emotional Intelligence in Negotiation and Conflict Resolution

Negotiation and conflict resolution are critical aspects of entrepreneurship, and emotionally intelligent leaders excel at navigating these situations with tact and diplomacy. By leveraging their emotional intelligence, these leaders can understand the emotions and perspectives of all parties involved, finding mutually beneficial solutions that drive positive outcomes.

Empathy is a crucial component of effective negotiation and conflict resolution. Emotionally intelligent entrepreneurs can put themselves in the shoes of others, understanding their needs, interests, and concerns. This deep understanding allows them to find common ground and develop solutions that address the needs of all parties involved. By demonstrating empathy and genuine concern for the well-being of others, these leaders can build trust and rapport, driving positive and collaborative outcomes.

Effective communication is another essential aspect of negotiation and conflict resolution. Emotionally intelligent entrepreneurs can use their social skills to engage in open and transparent dialogue, ensuring that all parties feel heard and understood. By actively listening to the concerns and perspectives of others, providing constructive feedback, and articulating their own needs and interests clearly, these leaders can find mutually beneficial solutions that drive positive outcomes.

Emotionally intelligent entrepreneurs also excel at managing their emotions during negotiation and conflict resolution. By recognizing and managing their emotional triggers, these leaders can stay calm and focused, making rational and thoughtful decisions. This composure not only enhances their decision-making abilities but also inspires confidence and trust among all parties involved, driving positive and collaborative outcomes.

11

Chapter 11: The Role of Emotional Intelligence in Personal Development

Personal development is a lifelong journey, and emotionally intelligent entrepreneurs understand the importance of continuous self-improvement. By leveraging their emotional intelligence, these leaders can cultivate a growth mindset, embracing challenges and learning opportunities with resilience and determination. This focus on personal development not only enhances their effectiveness as leaders but also drives long-term success and fulfillment.

Self-awareness is the foundation of personal development. Emotionally intelligent entrepreneurs can recognize their strengths and weaknesses, using this awareness to guide their self-improvement efforts. By identifying areas for growth and seeking out opportunities for learning and development, these leaders can continuously enhance their skills and capabilities. This commitment to self-awareness and self-improvement fosters a growth mindset, driving long-term success and resilience.

Self-regulation is another critical component of personal development. Emotionally intelligent entrepreneurs can manage their emotions effectively, preventing impulsive decisions and promoting thoughtful and strategic thinking. By cultivating self-discipline and resilience, these leaders can navigate challenges and setbacks with grace and determination. This focus on self-regulation not only enhances their effectiveness as leaders but also drives personal growth and fulfillment.

Emotionally intelligent entrepreneurs also prioritize the well-being of others in their personal development efforts. By cultivating empathy and social skills, these leaders can build strong relationships and foster a positive and supportive work environment. This focus on the well-being of others enhances their effectiveness as leaders and drives long-term success and fulfillment.

12

Chapter 12: Emotional Intelligence in Work-Life Balance

Work-life balance is essential for maintaining high levels of engagement and productivity, and emotionally intelligent entrepreneurs understand the importance of prioritizing their well-being and the well-being of their employees. By leveraging their emotional intelligence, these leaders can create a supportive and flexible work environment that promotes balance and fulfillment.

Self-awareness is a critical component of maintaining work-life balance. Emotionally intelligent entrepreneurs can recognize when their work demands are impacting their personal well-being and take proactive steps to address this imbalance. By setting boundaries and prioritizing self-care, these leaders can maintain high levels of energy and focus, driving long-term success and resilience.

Empathy is another essential aspect of promoting work-life balance. Emotionally intelligent entrepreneurs can understand the needs and preferences of their employees, creating a supportive and flexible work environment that accommodates their personal and professional responsibilities. By offering flexible work arrangements, promoting mental health initiatives, and encouraging regular breaks, these leaders can create a positive and inclusive work environment that enhances employee satisfaction and retention.

Effective communication is also crucial for maintaining work-life balance. Emotionally intelligent entrepreneurs can use their social skills to engage in open and transparent dialogue with their employees, addressing concerns and finding solutions that promote balance and well-being. This focus on effective communication fosters a culture of trust and collaboration, driving long-term success and fulfillment.

13

Chapter 13: Emotional Intelligence in Diversity and Inclusion

Diversity and inclusion are essential for driving innovation and business success, and emotionally intelligent entrepreneurs understand the importance of fostering an inclusive and supportive work environment. By leveraging their emotional intelligence, these leaders can create a culture that values and respects the unique perspectives and experiences of all team members, driving collaboration and innovation.

Empathy is a critical component of promoting diversity and inclusion. Emotionally intelligent entrepreneurs can understand and value the emotions and perspectives of their team members, creating a supportive and inclusive work environment. By demonstrating empathy and genuine concern for the well-being of others, these leaders can build trust and rapport, driving collaboration and innovation.

Effective communication is another essential aspect of promoting diversity and inclusion. Emotionally intelligent entrepreneurs can use their social skills to engage in open and transparent dialogue, ensuring that all team members feel heard and understood. By actively listening to the concerns and perspectives of others, providing constructive feedback, and articulating their own needs and interests clearly, these leaders can create a positive and inclusive work environment that drives collaboration and innovation.

Emotionally intelligent entrepreneurs also prioritize the well-being of all team members in their diversity and inclusion efforts. By promoting mental health initiatives, offering flexible work arrangements, and encouraging regular breaks, these leaders can create a supportive and inclusive work environment that enhances employee satisfaction and retention. This focus on the well-being of others not only enhances their effectiveness as leaders but also drives long-term business success and sustainability.

14

Chapter 14: Emotional Intelligence in Ethical Decision-Making

Ethical decision-making is a critical aspect of entrepreneurship, and emotionally intelligent leaders understand the importance of aligning their values with their actions. By leveraging their emotional intelligence, these leaders can navigate complex ethical dilemmas with integrity and transparency. This commitment to ethical decision-making not only enhances their credibility as leaders but also drives long-term business success and sustainability.

Self-awareness is a key component of ethical decision-making. Emotionally intelligent entrepreneurs can recognize their values and principles, using this awareness to guide their decision-making processes. By staying true to their values and maintaining a strong sense of integrity, these leaders can make ethical decisions that benefit their organization and stakeholders. This commitment to self-awareness and integrity fosters a culture of trust and accountability, driving long-term success.

Empathy is another crucial aspect of ethical decision-making. Emotionally intelligent entrepreneurs can understand and consider the emotions and perspectives of all stakeholders, ensuring that their decisions are fair and balanced. By putting themselves in the shoes of their employees, customers, and partners, these leaders can anticipate the potential impact of their decisions and make choices that are considerate and ethical. This empathetic approach to decision-making enhances trust and collaboration, driving positive outcomes.

Transparency and honesty are essential components of ethical decision-making. Emotionally intelligent entrepreneurs prioritize open communication and ensure that their actions align with their words. By being transparent about their decision-making processes and acknowledging their mistakes, these leaders can build trust and credibility with their stakeholders. This honesty and accountability create a culture of trust, where employees feel confident in their leaders' ability to make ethical decisions.

15

Chapter 15: The Impact of Emotional Intelligence on Organizational Change

Organizational change is a constant in the business world, and emotionally intelligent entrepreneurs are uniquely equipped to navigate these transitions with grace and resilience. By leveraging their emotional intelligence, these leaders can manage the emotional impact of change, fostering a sense of stability and trust within their organization. This ability to lead through change not only enhances their effectiveness as leaders but also drives long-term business success and adaptability.

Self-awareness is a critical component of leading organizational change. Emotionally intelligent entrepreneurs can recognize their own emotions and reactions to change, using this awareness to manage their stress and maintain their composure. By staying calm and focused, these leaders can make rational and thoughtful decisions, even in the face of uncertainty. This composure not only enhances their decision-making abilities but also inspires confidence and trust among their team members.

Empathy is another crucial aspect of leading organizational change. Emotionally intelligent entrepreneurs can understand and address the emotional impact of change on their employees, customers, and partners. By providing support and reassurance, these leaders can foster a sense of stability and trust, helping their organization navigate the challenges and uncertainties of change. This empathetic approach to change management enhances trust and loyalty, driving long-term success and adaptability.

Effective communication is essential for leading organizational change, and emotionally intelligent entrepreneurs excel at maintaining open and transparent communication with their stakeholders. By providing regular updates and addressing concerns promptly, these leaders can keep their teams informed and engaged, minimizing uncertainty and confusion. This proactive approach to communication fosters a sense of trust and collaboration, driving organizational resilience and adaptability.

16

Chapter 16: Emotional Intelligence in Strategic Planning

Strategic planning is a vital aspect of entrepreneurship, and emotionally intelligent leaders understand the importance of aligning their strategies with their values and goals. By leveraging their emotional intelligence, these leaders can create strategic plans that are informed, adaptable, and resilient. This focus on strategic planning not only enhances their effectiveness as leaders but also drives long-term business success and sustainability.

Self-awareness is a key component of strategic planning. Emotionally intelligent entrepreneurs can recognize their strengths and weaknesses, using this awareness to guide their strategic planning efforts. By leveraging their strengths and seeking support in areas where they may lack expertise, these leaders can create comprehensive and effective strategic plans. This commitment to self-awareness and continuous improvement fosters a growth mindset, driving long-term success.

Empathy is another crucial aspect of strategic planning. Emotionally intelligent entrepreneurs can understand and consider the emotions and perspectives of all stakeholders, ensuring that their strategic plans are fair and balanced. By putting themselves in the shoes of their employees, customers, and partners, these leaders can anticipate the potential impact of their strategies and make choices that are considerate and ethical. This empathetic approach to strategic planning enhances trust and collaboration, driving positive outcomes.

Adaptability is essential for effective strategic planning, and emotionally intelligent entrepreneurs excel at navigating change and uncertainty. By staying flexible and open to new ideas, these leaders can adjust their strategies as needed, ensuring that their plans remain relevant and effective. This adaptability not only enhances their decision-making abilities but also drives long-term business success and resilience.

17

Chapter 17: The Future of Emotional Intelligence in Entrepreneurship

The future of entrepreneurship is shaped by the evolving landscape of business and technology, and emotionally intelligent leaders are uniquely positioned to thrive in this dynamic environment. By leveraging their emotional intelligence, these leaders can navigate the complexities and uncertainties of the future, driving innovation, ethical leadership, and sustainable success.

The importance of emotional intelligence in entrepreneurship will continue to grow as the business world becomes increasingly interconnected and complex. Emotionally intelligent leaders who prioritize empathy, self-awareness, and ethical decision-making will be better equipped to build strong relationships, foster a positive organizational culture, and drive long-term success. This focus on emotional intelligence not only enhances their effectiveness as leaders but also creates a more inclusive and sustainable business environment.

Innovation will remain a critical driver of entrepreneurial success, and emotionally intelligent leaders will play a key role in fostering a culture of creativity and continuous improvement. By leveraging their emotional intelligence, these leaders can inspire their teams to think outside the box, embrace change, and push the boundaries of what is possible. This commitment to innovation and emotional intelligence will drive long-term business success and resilience.

Ethical leadership will also be essential for the future of entrepreneurship, as businesses face increasing scrutiny and accountability from stakeholders. Emotionally intelligent leaders who prioritize integrity, transparency, and social responsibility will be better positioned to build trust and credibility with their stakeholders. This focus on ethical leadership not only enhances their reputation but also drives long-term business success and sustainability.

In conclusion, emotional intelligence is a critical aspect of entrepreneurial success, and emotionally intelligent leaders are uniquely equipped to navigate the complexities and uncertainties of the future. By prioritizing empathy, self-awareness, ethical decision-making, and innovation, these leaders can create a positive and sustainable business environment, driving long-term success and fulfillment.

Book Description

The Emotionally Intelligent Entrepreneur: Blending Innovation, Culture, and Ethical Leadership is a comprehensive guide that explores the vital role of emotional intelligence in entrepreneurship. This book delves into the key components of emotional intelligence, including self-awareness, empathy, and effective communication, and demonstrates how these traits can enhance leadership, drive innovation, and foster a positive organizational culture.

Through 17 insightful chapters, the author, Emmanuel, provides practical strategies and real-world examples to help entrepreneurs navigate the complexities of the business world with grace and resilience. From ethical decision-making and strategic planning to crisis management and work-life balance, this book offers a roadmap for entrepreneurs to harness the power of emotional intelligence and achieve long-term success.

Whether you are an aspiring entrepreneur or a seasoned business leader, *The Emotionally Intelligent Entrepreneur* will inspire you to cultivate your emotional intelligence, embrace innovation, and lead with integrity. This book is a must-read for anyone seeking to build a thriving, sustainable, and ethical business in today's dynamic and interconnected world.

www.ingramcontent.com/pod-product-compliance
Lightning Source LLC
LaVergne TN
LVHW010441070526
838199LV00066B/6130